HAIR BOSS

A HAIRSTYLISTS' GUIDE TO OWNING THEIR CAREER

- - - - - - - - - - - -

JAMIE WILEY

Ordering Information:
Quantity sales. Special discounts are available on quantity purchases by corporations, associations, and others. For details, contact the publisher at the address above.

Printed in the United States of America

First Printing, 2018

Print ISBN: 978-1-54392-598-2

eBook ISBN: 978-1-54392-599-9

Dedications

To my husband Jonathan you are my constant steady star and without your light, love and laughter I would be lost.

To my children Cooper, Aubrey, and Madalynn my greatest works of art. Let this book be a reminder that no matter what happens in life you can have, be and do anything.

To my Dad and my Cindy, your steadfast Midwest ways have given me the humblest of roots that I carry deep within. Thank you.

To my siblings – Gabe, Courtney, Naomi and Nicole. Without the years of sibling rivalry, I wouldn't be the competitive person I am today. Thank you for that. Also, I love you. I don't say it nearly enough.

To my life long best friend Wojo. You have kept me grounded in a way no one else can. Our friendship has stood the test of time and distance. I am grateful to call you my person.

In loving memory of my mom, Cheri Lynn. She taught me so many lessons in life; but the greatest was on the day she departed and passed on. And that lesson was this; we only have one chance at this life. So, set aside the doubts, the fears and the baggage. Go after what sets your soul on fire and don't sweat the small stuff along the way. Remember just when the caterpillar thinks that it's over, it becomes a butterfly. So, close your eyes, trust the process and then fly. Thank you, mom, for giving me the courage to fly. This one is for you. I can't wait to tell you all about it someday.

Table of Contents

Preface

Greetings! My name is Jamie Wiley.

I am a trainer, educator, session stylist, and business owner but most importantly I am a stylist behind the chair. I have worked with thousands of professionals helping them to achieve higher levels of income, performance and growth. Through the years their secret weapon of success has come from the knowledge and application of HAIR BOSS; the same techniques you are about to discover in this book.

I am honored you have chose to embark on this journey and I'm excited for you to become a **HAIR BOSS.**

Now What?

How can I grow?

In cosmetology school, we build a foundation to a career, just like a foundation to a house must be completed before the walls and roof can go up. Cosmetology school, and the foundation we build there, set the beginning stage of where and how we want our career to progress. It is where we learn the basics—the bare minimum needed in order to get us ready to pass our state board exams. Getting a license is only the beginning of a successful career in hair, which means a career of learning. In the hair world, knowing the rules like the back of your hand is not just a requirement . . . owning those rules is vital. Once we master the rules, we can bend them like a true artist. This mastery of the rules is not optional; it is a necessity. If you don't know the basics, or how to use them, you will flounder quickly.

Those of us who seek continuing education throughout the entirety of our careers are the ones who fully reap the benefits. What are those benefits? Higher income, ideal hours, mentoring, a full clientele, and so much more.

Even seasoned stylists seek further education and inspiration 10, 20, and 30 years into their careers. Trends constantly change and progress as time goes on. Keeping up with those trends is imperative to having a great long-term career, one that satisfies you and your clients. The consequences of not continuing education are unpleasant and often fatal to a career: you can become stagnant, get bored, and face the possibility of burnout. Education keeps us inspired, motivated, and grounded as professionals and as artists who want to truly enjoy our careers.

How can I continue to grow?

Salons are increasingly selective in their pursuit of hiring talented hairdressers, especially those who are straight out of school. What some newcomers to the business may not realize is that finding a salon should be just as selective on their part as it is on the salons'. You are interviewing salons, just as much as they are interviewing you. Finding a salon that thrives on education is imperative. If the salon doesn't offer quarterly education, run. This is not the salon you want to work for. A salon that revolves around continuing education is where you will find the money makers, the ground breakers, the inventors, and the innovators of this industry. Those salons are where you want to be. If you are currently at a salon that does not offer education, this might be a conversation you want to have at your next one-on-one. You have a voice. You are someone who brings in revenue for the business. Your opinion matters.

With an emphasis on continuing education, you will grow at a rapid rate. The more you know, the more you can create and offer higher quality services to your guests. The more you offer, the more money you will make. And let's be honest—who doesn't dream of a career that gives financial freedom? A schedule that works for you. The creativity and energy to give quality services to your guests. All while reaping the benefits at the same time. It's a beautiful dance, and this book will teach you the steps. What to skip over, and what to pay special attention to.

Finding local education

The fastest and easiest way to take your career into your own hands is locating your nearest distributor store:

- SalonCentric
- State
- RDA
- Masello
- A&A

These top-notch establishments distribute brands on a large scale across the country and have stores in or near your city. These stores often host local and national talent educators in each brand. They are your ticket to the least expensive form of in-person education.

The types of education you will find are demonstrations, hands-in, and hands-on experiences.

Demonstrations are great because you can show up with a pen and paper, spend a few hours learning what your heart desires, and then leave. Hands-in is a class type that offers a hands-on experience while sharing tools and mannequins with two to four other attendees. And hands-on allows you to see a demonstration and then practice it immediately on an individual basis. Just you, your tools, and the mannequin. This type of education is the most effective. You are 12 times more likely to remember a new technique if you experience it for yourself during hands-on.

One thing I love about local education is meeting the educators. Take advantage of the opportunity to talk to and network with them. Get their social media and contact info for future endeavors. We will cover networking in more detail later. For now, remember that you never know the opportunities that will present themselves just by making a connection!

These store classes sometimes can be free or are offered at a very reasonable price, so keep a lookout for such events, especially in the spring and fall. These types of in-store offerings are amazing educational opportunities.

What's the best way to get salon education and support?

Now that you're at the perfect salon for you, one of the first things you'll want to do is watch the stylists. See who is skilled and successful at this craft. Who has the largest clientele? Who has a high retail-to-service percentage? Watch the ones who give exceptional service. Ask that team member if you can shadow them. It can be something as simple as watching them in action, or as full-bodied as a mentorship. Whatever you're comfortable with.

When I was in training, I was scared out of my mind. I quickly realized that I didn't truly know what I was getting myself into. So, I developed the sweep technique—I carried a broom around the salon. It was my excuse to watch the upper-level stylists while I swept up hair. We were told the break room was where careers go to die, but I didn't know where to be if I didn't have clients. No one tells you what to do or where to go. What I'm telling you is what I wish someone had told me at that point in my career.

I was attached to the broom. I would sweep as the senior staff cut. I kept to myself, making sure my presence did not interrupt the experience for the guest. This was my solution to get out of the back room and learn by watching those who were extremely successful in the salon. And it's a technique that still wins the day for newcomers. Sweep the hair. If you have a question, wait until the stylist is between clients and then ask. "So, I noticed you held the hair at this elevation . . . why?" or "You over-directed that section . . . what will it make the hair do?" You will learn at a supremely rapid rate when you watch others. You will learn what you like and also what you don't like.

When education becomes available, ask for what you really need. We often feel safe in our comfort zone, so we choose classes that are easy for us. But to truly push yourself, to grow, and to become a well-rounded hairdresser, you will be better off choosing classes that place you outside of your comfort zone.

One simple way to ensure your salon remains educated is to sell products. One reliable option for salons to earn more classes for their team is through product sales. Let your guests know that the products they buy from you will fund your continuing education. In return for their support through buying the quality product at your salon, they are supporting you so that you can serve them better! Most guests have no idea how our industry works. Let them know! They are more likely to be loyal and buy their haircare needs from you rather than online or at the supermarket (gasp!). One of the best ways to inform them is with a framed sign in a visible place that reads as follows:

"Thank you for purchasing your haircare needs with us. By doing so, you are funding higher education for our team. This education is to better serve you and bring you the latest and greatest in the industry. We appreciate your support."

I'm ready for something bigger.
How can I find brand-specific education?

Each distributor holds a yearly trade show that brings all of their brands to one location for two to three days of world-renowned education. This is where you will find the newest products and advancements in the industry. Evolving trends will be showcased and demonstrated for you so that you can take the latest back to the salon the very next day. This is a great place to find inspiration.

You'll never forget your first hair show as a hairdresser. Every show I attend teaches me something valuable. I leave a better person and a better hairdresser, whether I'm attending for personal education or if I'm working one. Being in a space with so much talent elevates you to another wavelength. You can feel the love, energy, and sheer talent emanating from the educators. It's contagious and will directly affect you behind the chair. The vast majority of Americans are unhappy with their jobs. Hairdressers are one of the lucky few professions that is made up of a large group of people who are passionate about what they do. Being a part of this profession, part of a group that loves what it does, is remarkable. Getting together under one roof to share ideas and learn from each other is indescribably amazing.

You can find these trade shows online or from your sales consultant at the salon. I like to mark my calendar for the year. Most distributors will post their show dates well in advance, so plan ahead and go with coworkers.

Attending every year is ideal as trends, content, and products change rapidly.

Why should I use social media education?

Social media is the fastest and easiest way to get in the know.
This is where hairdressers themselves are setting viral trends all
throughout the many social channels. You never know if something
that you do could go viral!

My favorite part about social channeling education is that you
get to do it anywhere, especially at home and in your jammies!

Our industry is visual. So, utilizing Instagram and YouTube to
catch up on techniques and trends is great. Just know that this type
of knowledge is quick and easy, and is sometimes viewed as micro-
waved (meaning, the quality is not ideal). Of course, we would all
much rather cook our meal in the oven, and eat meals made from
scratch, so be sure to balance the variety of educational avenues.
Mix hands-on experiences as well as social channels. We must try
not to rely solely on social media for education, and make sure we
experience fresh ideas first-hand.

By watching educators on their social channels, you will experience things in the moment. You can see into their world as an
educator, and they often share sneak peek info about which trends
are coming.

Where can I ground all this learning?

Back in the salon! When you have downtime, get your manne-
quin out. Some people think when they leave cosmetology school,
they will never have to see another mannequin again. Whoa! So
wrong. Mannequins give us a chance to play with ideas and test
out the new things we learn. With mannequins, we get to set up
at our station and practice the motions repetitively so that skills
become engrained, setting us apart. All the great hairdressers have

mannequins that they use to practice on. One of my mentors—an iconic hairdresser of our time—Ruth Roche, will practice doing a haircut (after learning it) seven or eight times before she will showcase it in public. This alone sets her apart. It makes her the icon that she is. She sets the standard high, becoming engrained so deeply in her content before actually doing a cut on a live model or client. And that standard shows. She would not be as good as she is without honing her craft on mannequins.

You can also use another hairstylist in the salon, to practice on each other. Or if you have a few sisters like I do, practice on them. (Sshh, don't tell them I used them for practice for years without their knowledge.)

Practice, practice, practice. Oh, and then practice some more. And when you feel like you have it down, practice it two more times. This is where a lot of hairdressers fall short. They aren't practicing enough. Our hands have to repeat a motion 20 times consecutively before that knowledge is engrained into us. Repetition improves learning. This is why hairdressers fall short in braiding. We try two or three times and give up. Keep going until it becomes second nature. Practice and repeat. Then execute.

How can I become bigger?

Alright! You're in this to win! You're ready to seek out specialties and certifications. Woot, woot! This is where you will set yourself above your peers. You will get instant credibility and recognition in the salon and from clients. A few ways you can set yourself apart is to become color certified. There are different certifications, depending on what color line and brand you use. They will be difficult, but that's what makes it prestigious! There are other certifications in extension work, design, straightening, balayage, etc. Find your tribe or brand, and look at their certifications. Pick the one you want to tackle first.

Guests love when they can say, "My hairdresser is certified in design, which is why my hair looks so amazing!" And when you speak to other hairdressers or salons, you're able to say I (and my team) are design certified. The credibility alone elevates you to the next level. Once you are certified, make sure you update your social platforms to reflect your newest attributes.

How do I become an educator?

You're ready for the big leap! The single most inspiring, and fastest, way to build yourself and your business is by joining a brand. Becoming the face of their products and education puts the force of their name behind you. Choose wisely.

Here are a few things to consider:

- Think about integrity. Do they do what they say?

- Is their brand healthy for hair and the environment?

- Will this brand protect MY health even after long-term exposure?

- Am I doing this for me?

- Am I willing to sacrifice time away from family and clients?

- Am I ready for the pressure?

- Am I ready to publicly speak?

- Am I ready for an adventure of a lifetime?

These are questions you must address. If all your answers are in line with a "yes," then you're ready to take the next big step in the dance of your career.

My journey as an educator is with Pureology, which has changed my life personally and professionally. I chose them because of their integrity and sustainability. Also, because the products are incredible. At my first hair show, I witnessed Pureology demand the attention of the attendees. The way they made the hair move and without (what seemed like) much effort. The way they spoke and how they were dressed. It really was as if the heavens opened up and said, "That's your tribe, Jamie."

So, I went home and looked into becoming a Pure artist. I sent in my application and video, and two weeks later I received an invitation for a phone interview. I had two more phone interviews after that. Then I was invited to induction in Santa Monica, California. Induction was four days of intense learning and training. Lots of tears and emotions I didn't expect. Afterwards we had one month to make a video that would be evaluated. It took another month after that to hear the results. And I received the call inviting me to be a part of the Pureology tribe.

That was seven years ago, and I have watched my career go places I never could have imagined for myself. I have traveled to incredible locations, and have met the most inspiring hairdressers and salon owners. I have worked events and assisted world-renowned hair icons. I've had opportunities present themselves through my brand, but also through the techniques I will teach you in this book. So, hold on, there's so much more to come!

When seeking out the brand you want to align yourself with, don't give up if it doesn't happen right away. I mean this with all of my heart. Don't let life get in the way of your goal. For some, it takes years to get picked up by a brand. But if it's truly in your soul, you will wait and try again and again until it happens. Then when it does, it will be worth the while!

HAIR BOSS HACK- Keep track of all that you do. Numbers in the salon, education, personal development, etc. Write down the month and year you attend all continuing education events. This will be ammunition for when you go for a raise or promotion within your salon and or apply to the brand to be an educator!

Know your worth -
Then add tax

How to choose a price point?

When choosing an initial salon to work at, look at their starting haircut prices. Do research, and lots of it. Find out what the average income is in the area where the salon is located. You want your haircuts to reflect the average income earner in the area. Getting a job at a salon with a higher income earning is a leg up for you as a stylist. Instead of starting at a lower haircut price and working years to gain a high price, starting out higher can take years off the chase for higher prices and more income.

This is what you will be making from the get-go. So, choosing a lower price point of $10 to $20 will take you a bit of time to work your way up the ladder. But if you start at $34, you've cut your time in half by starting higher. I know professionals who will travel an hour one way to be at a higher end salon with high-paying guests. Envisioning what you want your ideal client to look like, how much you'd like them to spend, and how often you want them to visit all starts with the location of the salon.

Another consideration is, what feels right for you? For some hairdressers, lower price point salons are a perfect fit, while others want to service mostly color clients working with three to four clients a day. Personal preference is never a bad thing. We will break down the numbers later on to show what both of those earnings will look like.

When should I increase my prices?

The moment you are hired, find out the system. Are there level increases, or fee increases, or both? Learn the ins and outs of the system. That way you know exactly what you have to do in order to make your way to the top of the ladder.

Study those who are putting in the most effort in the salon. Ask them how long it took them to get to the level they are at. Ask them what to expect along the way and to share any tips that they can.

Once you have built a foundation and are maintaining at that level for at least three months' minimum, you are ready for an increase. This is a good rule of thumb for stylists who are hungry for growth. After you have maintained your numbers, speak to your managers and ask if they agree upon your next move toward growth. One of the well-known systems in the industry is Summit Salons. They break everything down for you to understand, track, and stay in motion to making a desirable living.

When you certify yourself, or take continuing education, you are able to charge more. This is where stylists lose the big picture. They often never know when to raise their prices, or they feel obligated to remain at the same price for years and years. When you raise your prices, you will lose some clients. This is a natural and normal part of growth. Just remember, there are guests out there who won't even consider seeing you unless you are at the new fee. You will attract a whole new group of clients just from your higher price alone. These astute clients know that hairdressers who charge a certain amount have put in the time, effort, and commitment to earn that rate, and that these stylists have received the right education to charge a particular rate. And they can expect the highest service in that salon, which is what they want for their money. So, you will lose a few clients, but gain more in return. TRUST THE PROCESS.

How do you add value to your service?

Do you want to know the fastest way to grow your business?

Come on, Jamie! Of course, I do!

The fastest way to grow your business is to set your salon apart from others, and to set yourself apart from other stylists within your salon.

So how do we set ourselves apart?

By fulfilling the customer's INTANGIBLE expectations, we create an emotional experience for them.

INTANGIBLE expectations, for the guest, includes *feeling*:

- Welcomed
- Like a friend
- Appreciated
- Cared for through presentation
- Cared for through appearance
- Cared for through cleanliness
- Connected

Feeling welcomed. Is the guest properly welcomed? Not just "Hi, how are you?" when she walks in. "How are you?" in our society is an empty greeting. You aren't really asking someone how she is, you are just greeting her. Instead open with, "Welcome to _____Salon, can I take your coat?" This is a true, genuine welcome into the space. Then you take it further and ask if she would like a drink. If she is a new guest, give her a tour. And let her know how long her provider will be. Treat the guest the same as if you invited someone new to your home. In order for her to feel welcome, she will want to know where to use the bathroom, be offered something to drink, and know how long she will be waiting until something happens.

Feeling like a friend. How is the staff treating every guest, and not just their own guest? Sixty percent of guests throughout the industry feel like they are being treated impersonally due to a lack of friendliness.

Feeling appreciated. Are you grateful for their visit? Do you thank them for their loyalty? We often miss this emphasis. Thank them for choosing you and being a part of your business, every time they come.

Feeling cared for through presentation. How was each step of the service presented? How are you presenting products to them? How is the presentation of your tools and the back bar? All of these factors weigh in on the overall presentation of the salon.

Feeling cared for through appearance. Does your guest feel cared for through your appearance? Being in the beauty industry, our guests look to us to show the way. They look at our appearance first. We represent what guests come to us to achieve. You have a seven-second window to make a good first impression, and your appearance plays a large part in that.

Feeling cared for through cleanliness. A lack of cleanliness is the number two reason a guest will not return to a salon. Even if she loves her hairstyle and the hairdresser, if the bathroom is a mess the whole experience suffers for the guest. Guests do not feel cared for if any part of the salon is dirty or messy. Cleanliness shows care for the client's experience and comfort.

Feeling connected. Finally, do your guests feel an emotional connection during their time in your space? Do they feel connected to you or to the salon in some way?

There are two things that customers cannot forgive when visiting and seeking to fulfill their INTANGIBLE expectations. These deal breakers are poor service and inauthentic communication.

80% percent: The percentage of service providers who think they give great service.

8% percent: The percentage of customers who think they get great service.

Offer the little things; these are big in the world of your guests. Each detail of the experience in your salon can turn the guest's experience from mediocre to exceptional.

Another way to create a connection is through retail. As human beings, we often think of sales as something negative. When we shift our perspective about sales to advice, it changes the game of retail. We are here to help our guests with their wants, desires, and needs in the salon and at home. You are offering your valuable, professional advice and educating them. You are a source of vital information that will improve their lives. More advice = more sales.

If they don't purchase product from you, but you know they will love it, hand them a sample of that product to take home with them and try for free.

Fifty-six percent of guests who try a sample product come back for the full size!

BUT, hand the product to them with both hands, look them in the eye, and say,

"I understand you aren't taking the full-size home today, but I know this will help with the issues you were telling me about. And you will love it! So, this is for you. Please use it, and let me know what you think. I want you to be able to recreate the style that we did today at home, and it'll be easier with this product here."

The personal details in this gesture will set the experience above and beyond. They will know that you truly care about them and aren't in it just for the sale.

Other ways to add value . . .

Think about one of the biggest companies in the world . . . . Apple. When you walk into an Apple store, how far do you get before someone greets you? Two or maybe three steps, right? There are things to touch and play with and experience all around. Once you speak to the advisor, do you find yourself having a conversation, or do you feel you are fighting off a pushy salesman?

It's a conversation! They truly want to know what your lifestyle is and how they can better serve you. Help you. Also, those Apple employees aren't salespeople. They truly love the industry they work in, and dare I call them nerds, but they are. They didn't wake up and say, "I can't wait to sell stuff today." No. They woke up passionate about technology. They have guided you through the experience of finding the technology that will make your life better, and they make suggestions along the way. They are eager to educate you about your new device so that you can use it to its full potential at home. Then you're ready to check out. Do you go to a register? No! The register comes to you. They ring you up right where you are standing. And if you purchased something, they bring it to you already wrapped and in a bag. It is completely customized to the client. Our industry could learn a lot from the Apple model of selling products. Sales is less about money, and more about offering advice to help people.

Another way to add value to your clients' experience is by hitting their five senses.

- Sight
- Smell
- Touch
- Taste
- Hearing

SIGHT

How does the salon look when you walk in the door, what is the FIRST impression the guest has? This goes back to cleanliness.

SMELL

Does the salon have a fragrance? Do you have aromatherapy in the reception area? Do you have a candle or a fragrance infused into your airflow? This will set the stage for the entire visit. If you've ever been to Las Vegas, most of the higher-end hotels and casinos infuse their air with scented aromatherapies. It conveys a sense of belonging and can evoke warm memories, relaxing the body and mind. It creates a desirable atmosphere in which people want to stay. Studies have shown that the use of orange extract encourages shoppers to spend 20 percent more than they normally would. In our industry, we want to put our guest's mind at ease. Studies show that 70 percent of guests feel anxious when they go to a hair salon for the first time. Using the sense of smell to ease their minds will help them enjoy a relaxing experience.

TOUCH

Can they experience the products that the stylists are putting in their hair or on their face or nails? Having a station that allows the guests to open, smell, touch, and look at things creates a sensory rich experience. They will be more apt to buy something that they get to play with first.

TASTE

Do you offer refreshments? Mints, treats, candies, cookies? I worked in a spa salon in Burnsville, Minnesota, that offered chocolate-covered strawberries and other treats on Saturdays. And EVERYONE knew it and booked on Saturdays. They wanted that experience! It sets you apart from the salon down the street, and guests will come back again and again. The drinks you offer can also provide a variety of taste experiences. Consider offering more than only water or coffee. Perhaps you can have a sampler of tea flavors on hand as well.

HEARING

What kind of music do you have playing in the background? Is it relaxing? Uplifting? Fun? Is it too loud? Too quiet? Does it create an atmosphere that reflects the salon? Do your guests like it? Ask!

Do you read your guests' body language? Can you tell when they want to talk and when they want to relax? The shampoo bowl and head massage is one of the key places we should be quiet and let the guest enjoy the experience. An alarming 70 percent of guests will not return if the experience at the shampoo bowl is subpar. Think about that. So, our effort in the guest's experience at the shampoo bowl needs to be above and beyond. This is the time to meet all your client's intangible expectations.

When something amazing happens to us, we tell our friends. Our guests do the same thing. And a client recommendation is **50 times better than a paid advertisement!**

So, all of these tactics of enriching your guests' sensory enjoyment while in your salon will create an ideal atmosphere and add value to your services. Your guest will be happy and become loyal. A happy and loyal guest creates more happy and loyal guests.

What's TIG versus TIS?

Time in grade versus time in service.

Before my hairdressing days, I served in the US Army. This term stems from that perspective. The Army has what is called time in service (TIS) and time in grade (TIG). Time in service is total accumulated time served. Time in grade is how long you have been in that rank or role. For time in grade, we will refer to it as time spent in a role or level. Spending a certain amount of time in grade, in a certain role before moving on to the next, will showcase your education, talent, and ability.

For example, let's say Gabe has been in the industry for 50 years but hasn't taken a single class. His coworker Nicole has been in the industry for two years and engages in continuing education weekly. Which one makes for a more well-rounded hairdresser? The one with weekly education for two years! That means time in grade trumps time in service.

This is an area in our industry where ego can create tension. Some hairdressers may gloat about their time in service or time with a brand or salon and may pass judgment on hairdressers with fewer years in service. But what they don't take into account is their time in grade. What have they done with their time? Have they taken risks? Certified themselves? Engaged in higher education? Traveled for new opportunities? Found a mentor that will make them better, even after decades in service?

Your time in grade is more important than time in service. And don't let anyone make you feel a certain way about how long you have been in the industry. More than likely your time in grade is more than theirs!

How valuable is your time?

Time is the most valuable thing we possess. It is estimated that 85 percent of Americans hate what they do for a living. They are literally committing spiritual suicide. The vast majority of us in the hair industry chose to be here because of true passion. We are among the 15 percent of Americans who can say we love what we do. We spend our time making others feel good about themselves, which is one of the most rewarding aspects of our job.

Something else about time? Once it's gone, we can never have it back. When we talk about charging for time in this industry, it is truly the key to our livelihood. For example, charging by time rather than by service will help you increase your bottom line. There may be certain services that you will charge by the hour, such as extensions, on-scalp braiding, color corrections, and vivid color services. Those tend to take hours at a time. It's equivalent to tattoo artists; they charge by the hour because of their artistic talent. We are in that same realm.

When we use other people's time, our time becomes even more valuable. When you are away from your spouse, children, family, loved ones for a work assignment, we must take into account the time lost with them. Particularly special times, such as on holidays, anniversaries, or weekends are often in demand because hairdressers work ridiculous hours. Nevertheless, we must know that our time is the greatest value and asset, and we must charge accordingly based on that value.

Now we also need to know when to hold them and when to fold them when it comes to your time value. There are times when we are overworked, underpaid, stressed, sad, and burnt out. Because let's face it—at times we can be glorified therapists. We share in conversations about our guests' most intimate and important life experiences: marriages, divorces, funerals, weddings, birthdays, you name it. We stand with them through their highs and lows. Figuring out how much our time is worth is part of deciding what and how to charge.

What are your strengths?

Know your weakness, but play to your strengths. We all have weaknesses, but we don't have to put them on display. Instead put your strengths under the light for all to see! As a hairdresser, we want to focus on our strengths. Build a book that focuses on that. If you are an amazing colorist, you should be upselling color during every single haircut in your chair. Eventually, you want your books to be primarily color. If finishing and upstyling are your strengths, then proms and weddings should be your focus. Eventually, you want to build those weekends and pack them full.

If you want to strengthen your weaknesses, that is when we turn to the P word! Practice. Practice. Practice. If you've ever watched a skilled hairdresser at work, know that you are watching the end result of years of practice. Stylists at the top of the field got there from years of practice in private in order for them to perform effortlessly in public.

Call your strengths and weaknesses out to your salon team. Share out loud as a team: I'm strong here, while another team member is strong in this area. Take turns comparing assessments. Then work TOGETHER to build the team up. If you have to step away to help another hairdresser, do it. They will then do that for you when you need it. A well-oiled salon team is apparent when it's all-hands-on-deck. The guest sees this teamwork and appreciates it because it's proof that the guest's experience is more important than any stylist's ego.

How do I over deliver and under promise?

NEVER PROMISE RESULTS BEHIND THE CHAIR.

This is a rule that is not easy to master.

Hair makes up so much chemistry. Then we add in hormones, medications, illnesses, and many other factors that figure into the outcome of hair color. Often stylists get themselves in hot water when they say that they can accomplish something and then chemistry takes over. We scratch our heads, wondering what went wrong. So many factors can lead to the unexpected end result.

Mastering the color wheel and hair color takes years and loads of experience. This is why under promising but over delivering is key.

Examples of verbiage to use:

"This is our goal, but we may end up with a different result because of (xyz). Are you ok with that?"

"This may be a work in progress. It may not be something we can get you to today."

Let the guest know this in advance. Have the guest repeat it back to you, so that there is no confusion. This will eliminate redo's or the guest being unnecessarily disappointed and leaving negative feedback.

You may want to consider using a disclosure form if you are not sure about the outcome. The guest will sign the form, ensuring that communication has been as clear as possible about expectations and promises. These disclosures can say anything you'd like. Most of them are about the outcome of the color. Some hairdressers will even have guests sign a disclosure form before beginning services if they are expected to spend over a certain dollar amount. Another time when such a form is helpful is when a guest isn't taking color-safe shampoo home. Then the hairdresser cannot guarantee the color work from fading. Another time when it's recommended to introduce a disclosure form with a guest is if you have that gut feeling that the person sitting in your chair isn't honest and trustworthy . . . you know the sketchy type. Have them sign a form for your protection. Because as much as we like to trust all people, we do need to protect ourselves! More salons are using disclosure forms with each and every guest, each and every time, to protect the interest of both the client and the stylist. Utilizing the form in this way, across the board, takes away the necessity of having to assess each person who sits in your chair, and each situation that you find yourself facing. A disclosure form is a type of insurance for the stylist and client. It's a contract of communication.

Another important safeguard for a hairdresser is insurance. Whether you own or rent a space or a chair, insurance is a must. Note that if you are an employee under management, you will be covered by the owner's insurance.

Communication/Consultation is key.

With 7 out of 10 guests feeling anxious when they walk in the door, when do you think we can put their minds fully at ease? Yes, you're right! During the consultation. If anything, negative happens during the service or post service, it can 99 percent of the time be linked back to what was communicated during the consultation. This portion of our service is the most important and critical moment for a satisfied outcome, but too often this moment is often rushed through.

A good rule of thumb for the consult:

60 percent of the time: the guest speaks

30 percent of the time: the stylist speaks

10 percent of the time: silence

Asking different types of questions during the consult will allow for the guest to speak 60 percent of the time. So, what kinds of questions should we ask during the consultation?

Note: "What are we doing today?"
IS NOT A CONSULTATION.

Consultation Questions:

- **What's the goal with your hair?**

- **How do you wear your hair on a daily basis?**

- **What kind of occupation do you have? Are there limitations or restrictions on how you can style your hair for your job?**

- **When was the last time you loved your style?**

- **What is the comfort level of styling your hair?**

- **What does a good hair day look like for you?**

- **How do you feel about your natural texture or curls?**

- **Tell me a time you got your hair cut and you were unhappy with it.**

- **Tell me a time you got your hair cut and you were very happy with it.**

- **What life events do you have coming up this year that we need to prepare for? Wedding, vacation, pregnancy, birthday?**

- **If I could share some techniques on how to style your hair, would you be interested?**

- **If I could show you the products that you need based on what you have told me, would you be interested?**

Listen for the key indicators when they are telling you about their wants, desires, and needs. This might be when they get excited. They may show you a picture. Watch for their face to light up and they get happy just talking about the vision they have. These key indicators will help you guide the outcome.

Finally, you want to repeat back to them what they said and what you got out of it to make sure that you are both on the same page.

Once this communication is complete, then you show the breakdown of pricing. Present what each service will cost separately, and then give the total. If they are getting a promotional service or first-time guest gift, show that as well. They will be at ease knowing what it costs right from the start. You don't want your client to be nervous and uncertain about the total price the entire time the service is performed, or for the price to consist of a guessing game at the end.

Mastering the art of the consultation can take your skill set to the next level.

HAIR BOSS HACK- 90 percent of your retail sales happen during the consultation.

How do I build my brand so that the money follows?

Stay on top of your game. Have a plan. Write that plan down. There is something about putting your goals on paper and giving it to the universe to deliver. Then, be patient. Wait with expectancy, knowing that your number will be called if you keep putting in the work. The universe will deliver, and often it will deliver something even better than what you could have imagined. When you know you are close to a promotion, you will work harder to get there. When you know your goals will become reality, you push to see it manifest.

An analogy that has stuck with me for years is the captain-less ship. Pretend you are on a beautiful ship, with lots of sunscreen, delicious food, and plenty of fancy drinks, but your captain has no destination. You just float along the ocean, aimlessly. The first few days might not be so bad, but after you drift aimlessly for days, weeks, and months, without a destination in sight, the days become daunting, despite the lovely distractions of creature comforts. You are lost, and you have no way of getting home or anywhere else for that matter. As humans, we lose hope and start to shut down, no matter how beautiful the view may be at the moment. This is our life without a plan. It is proven that humans need progress to be happy. Any kind of progress . . . just as long as we are moving forward toward something we value. A destination is necessary for value. A destination is our goal.

Now imagine you are on the same boat, but this time your captain has the destination locked in. You set off toward your final port. There may be rough seas ahead, and it might take you longer than expected to arrive, but as long as you are making progress every day toward that set location, you are on your way. If we do this in our life and career, and make progress every day, no matter how small, we will achieve our goals and ultimately create a feeling of fulfillment. A satisfaction of purpose and value of effort that cannot exist without a goal. This brings us happiness deep within. When our boat reaches its port, we then set another destination and continue the journey. As a hairdresser and a human being, we need to set goals to grow and flourish.

I watched a fellow hairdresser perform at a level 3 while receiving the benefits of a level 2. This went on for two years. It made no sense! She just never asked to go to level 3. Even when it was brought up, she wasn't ready for that level yet. What she didn't realize is that she was missing so much money and opportunity. The obstacle was that she didn't have a plan. She didn't realize how she had gotten to level 3 when she wasn't ready, and ultimately turned it down for two years. She grew into the role and eventually took the promotion. But a dream without a plan is just that, a dream. If she had written down her dream from Day One, she would have been ready to accept the reality of it when it happened. Don't wait to set your goal. You don't have to be there before you realize you want to get there. Dream it first. Write it down. Set your intention. Don't run or hide from it! Embrace it when it comes. Set a new goal.

Once you hit it your goal, make sure you ask for the promotion! Immediately. Call your manager or text in that moment in that day. Say, "Can we meet tomorrow? . . . I have some great news!" This will show initiative and prove that you have been tracking, working, and waiting for your time and that it's finally here! CELEBRATE!

Often times we don't ask for opportunities or gifts in our life because we are afraid to step outside of our comfort zone. Fear will shut us down and keep us trapped in complacency. Then we eventually become resentful at ourselves and others. So, look fear in the face and step toward it. In that moment, something amazing will happen—fear will disappear.

When should I add another layer?

There comes a time when your uncomfortable situations and tasks are no longer uncomfortable. You feel safe and secure, you have a routine, and you crush it every day. You are on autopilot. Nothing is scary anymore. This is the moment when your comfort zone has become *too* comfortable. This is a tell-tale sign that it's time to grow! A badass hairdresser will find the next thing that makes her uncomfortable, and she will go after it. That is the moment when you know you should add another layer to your skills as a hairdresser.

What's next after a full book?

Congrats! You are fully booked!! For some, it takes a year. For others, it takes 10 years or longer to achieve this goal. Regardless of how long it takes, it feels amazing! CELEBRATE!

Now, don't get too comfortable because there is room for more growth. I know you didn't think it would be possible, but here are some industry secrets about life after a full book.

Move guests around and make room for higher paying guests. Yep, that's right. You will have to give low-paying guests to someone else in order to open your books to high-paying guests. Think about it. You have high-paying guests. Don't you want your ENTIRE book to be full of those guests? So, start by giving those guests your prime-time spots on your books—nights and week-ends. Or times that they prefer. Then, bump your lower paying guests to the times that aren't priority. If you are feeling up to the challenge, give your low-ticket guests to another hairdresser to open your books for another high-paying color guest. BOOM, this is where you take your game from above average to elite!

At this point, you should have the "no apologies, thank you . . . next" mentality. It's not personal; it's business. Our guests forget after a while that this is our livelihood, but we must never forget it if we take our careers and our professional well-being seriously. When you break up with a client or offer him to another hairdresser, he may feel hurt. But keep it strictly business. Be polite and kind, but be firm.

If you have clients who are challenging to handle, requiring more time or effort than they are worth, consider bumping them or passing them to a colleague. These are a few scripts to use to send them on their way.

"I've been giving our relationship some thought, and after looking through our history, I've noticed a pattern that you have not been happy on several occasions. After giving this some thought, I don't think I am the stylist to suit your needs."

"Your appointments are proving to be far more stressful than I'm allowing myself to deal with, and I will no longer be providing any future hair services to you."

"I am grateful that you have been my client for so many years. At this time, however, I'd like to open my book to more color guests. I'd like to recommend _____, who is fully aware of our service and she is happy to take you on as a client."

How to sharpen your craft?

It takes 10,000 hours to master a single skill in your craft. That's a lot of hours! And as hairdresser, we have a lot of skills we need to know, do, and master to be well rounded. This can be overwhelming. To think of it in these terms, it seems it will take a lifetime to master our craft.

One of the best pieces of advice I ever received was this: Decide what you want to be remembered for. If someone wrote a biography about my career, what is the first thing I would want to be remembered by? Pick that skill to master first. Then go from there.

Choose one skill set and work on that over and over again until it's sharp and ready to use. Then move on to the next. Make a list of most important to least, according to my desires and goals. (Perms are at the bottom of my list. LOL.)

When do I know if I'm settling for less than I deserve?

The first salon I worked at had me in an associate program that they developed themselves. The thing is, I was the test pilot for the program. I was working for commission, but my haircut prices were $5. Yes, I was making commission on $5 haircuts because I was an associate. I wasn't paid a wage or any other compensation. I did this for nine months. I was young, naive, and thought that I had to put in the legwork to get to the good stuff. I just really had no clue.

I was a model worker. I showed up early, stayed late, did everything that was asked of me. They gave me homework, I did it. They were condescending and catty, and I took it like a champ. For nine months. And as a new hairdresser, I thought that this was the dues I had to pay. This salon did not have education, and I craved it. So, I paid for a hands-on ticket to Nick Arrojo. Easily more money than I had made the entire time in the industry at this salon. I met other professionals and asked how their journey was going. I quickly realized I was the glorified janitor at my current salon. I cleaned the bathroom, kitchen, dispensary, and reception area far more than I did hair. And I realized this is NOT THE NORM. I was crushed. I had wasted valuable time.

I met a salon manager at that program, and she offered me an interview at her flagship salon, which was bringing in $1 million a year. I took the offer, went to the interview, and got the job. Went back to my salon, walked in the door . . . they handed me a list of things the salon needed cleaned that day. I handed it back and said, "I'm going to a salon that will value my potential." They called me names and tried to put it back on me. They said I couldn't leave after how much they had invested in me.

Looking back now I realize that the lesson of those nine months was hard, but it set me up for the rest of my career. Time is something when it is gone you can never get back. Although I wasted time at that salon the value is in the lesson. If it's not ethical then we shouldn't settle for less than what we deserve. So my hopes in telling this story is that you know that you have endless possibility. If you feel in your gut that a salon isn't right for you, then it's not. Listen to that small voice. It's usually always right. Follow your instinct and go after what you envision and deserve.

What's my value?

Our value comes from time. How much is your time worth? How many years of experience do you have? How much advanced education have you attended? This goes back to the previous section on TIG versus TIS. Time is our value.

One of my favorite messages comes from F. Scott Fitzgerald:

For what it's worth: it's never too late or, in my case too early to be whoever you want to be. There's no time limit, stop whenever you want. You can change or stay the same, there are no rules to this thing. We can make the best or worst of it. I hope you make the best of it. And I hope you see things that startle you. I hope you feel things you never felt before. I hope you meet people with a different point of view. I hope you live a life you're proud of. If you find that you're not, I hope you have the courage to start all over again.

These words speak to the soul. Because we all give ourselves excuses. "I'm too old, I'm too young, I have kids, I'm getting married, I don't have time for that." Excuses can make us feel better about not pursuing the dream that sets our soul on fire. Once you let go of the excuses, that's when you realize your time is worth its weight in gold. Charge what you're worth, and don't apologize for it. There will be people who don't agree. That is fine. This isn't their journey. It wasn't given to them; it was given to you. And your time is worth it. Charge for it.

There are plenty of professions that require a license that charge for time. Doctors, dentists, surgeons, etc. And we have no problem paying for their expertise and time. What is the difference for a hair-dresser? The guest comes to us for our artistry, skill, expertise, and trained professionalism. All of these are wrapped up in our time.

Everyone is different. Charging $10 for a haircut is not a bad thing. If that's what you believe you are worth, then go for it! Charging $500 for a haircut is also not a bad thing. We are all different, all on different levels and phases of our journey and there is enough to go around for everyone. Just make sure that you are happy and fulfilled with the value that you bring and compensate for that accordingly.

How do I get guests to rebook every time?

The art of rebooking. We hear it every day. We are asked, "Did you rebook them?" After years of this pressure, we begin to hate the term. Especially if we are on numbers and need to make a certain rebook each day. So, whether you love rebooking or love to hate it, let's look at it once again. But this time, anew.

Rebooking is a skill. The best advice I ever received was to tease the guest. By talking about the next time, they come in. Suggest a subtle shift in their color formula or recommend bangs, or a gloss, etc. Something that shows that you are invested in them and looking toward the future and what is next for them. They appreciate the effort, your interest in them, and the attention, and you get them excited! They will rebook, and most likely will rebook a week or two sooner because they are looking forward to putting into action your recommendation!

Discounts versus promotions?

When we first start out in the industry, it's easy to give discounts. It's an effective way to get new guests into our chairs. Yet we want to send the right message to guests from the start. Offer a promotion instead of a discount.

What's the difference? By giving discounts, you send a message that you aren't confident in your work and your skill. It also shows that you are willing to sell yourself short by discounting. Then it happens again and then again. Then you have a book of discounted services, and the people in your chair want that level of service you gave the first time at the discounted rate, all the time. There is a built-in disappointment for the client after the first service. Focus on your promotions instead of discounting.

If a guest asks for a discount, offer them different options. Price out what they can afford and see what works with their budget. All of this breakdown of price points and offerings should take place during the consultation. Let them know what each service costs. If you come to a total that is too much for the client, then you can adjust their services accordingly.

Gaining Ideal Clients

How can I build a strong clientele?

Now more than ever our guests and future guests are seeking EXPERIENCES rather than the average hair session. They seek connection and meaning. They want to be heard, understood, and appreciated. By seeking to understand our clients' emotions, we create a connection. When we create a connection, we create an experience. When truly giving a memorable experience to your guests, you will average a 70 percent return rate. Right now, the average return rate for salons is 30 percent. Consider that: fulfilling your clients' emotional expectations makes a 40 percent difference in return. The number is staggering because the expectation is critical.

What's the best way to create high retention values and create an experience for the guest?

Greet them by name with a smile and firm handshake. Make eye contact and speak with a soothing voice. This will make them feel comfortable and welcome. Remember, 70 percent of guests are anxious when coming to the salon. We want to alleviate that anxiety from the moment they open the door.

Give them a tour and point out the restrooms. Introduce them to the owner or manager. That way they feel like part of the family, and the owner/manager can thank them at the BEGINNING of the service for their choice in coming to the salon.

Give them a thorough consultation. This is KEY. See the section on consultations in this book for knock-out questions to ask. Do this for old and new guests alike. Consult every time. Then offer your personal, professional recommendations for a new style or color, etc. By recommending and educating your client, you show that you truly care.

Invite them back and prebook with them while they are processing their color. This is also when you will be collecting products that you recommended for them during the consultation so that the products are ready when the guest is ready to check out.

Finally, check up on them after the service, by text, email, or even a phone call. Follow up to make sure they are happy with how the service went. Especially if they made a drastic change! I'll even tell them when they leave that I will be checking in with them. That is an example of a connection level of service that goes above and beyond in fulfilling emotional expectations!

Meet their basic human needs. For example, if it's lunch time and you are ordering food, see if they would like anything. Or if they are having a bad day, acknowledge it with empathy and let them know you are going to take care of them. When we acknowledge basic human needs, guests feel like they matter (because they do!).

When implementing these strategies, not only will you build a book quickly, you will build it with ideal clients that have an emotional connection to you or your salon. It makes this journey that much more special. They will take care of you just as much as you take care of them.

How to attract high-spending guests?

This is what high-spending guests want:

- Exceptional service
- Prompt response on inquiries
- Knowing the benefits
- The feeling of being special to your business
- Expectations met or exceeded

Going ABOVE AND BEYOND?

Have you ever heard that people buy people? This mentality boils down to connection. Everything that we have been talking about is connected to connection. Now we need to take it to the next level!

Give your clients the "highlight of their day" experience. Aim to be the best part of their day. So much so that they leave and tell everyone they know or see that day about you! They write about you on Facebook and social media.

Find your WOW factor. Everyone is different, so each of us will wow in our own way. But I can tell you that a huge part of going above and beyond is if your guest can tell if you LOVE what you do. That you are passionate and you are in it for them and not the money. Connect, create an experience, and you will exceed your guest's expectations and gain a long-lasting client.

Why do I want to chart my numbers?

The old mentality that this is a profession that we do until we grow up, or find something better, is gone! In this industry, there are hairdressers that make six-figure salaries (and more). And I'm not just talking about celebrity hairdressers. I'm talking about the everyday hairdresser from Minnesota working four days a week with a $55 haircut who is making six figures.

It's all about having those goals, the directions, and a plan to get there. Would you like to know the directions?

Awesome! Keep reading!!

You will need a pen and paper. Go get them. I'll wait here.

How much do you want/need to gross per year?

Select a number

Divide that number by:

How many days in the year you work

(This may vary depending on sick days/vacation days.)

This number will show you your daily total goal.

Break down that number based on your prices (you will see how many haircuts, colors, etc. you need to do in order to hit that goal).

Anything you don't hit on a certain day you can roll over and divide by how many days are left in the week or month.

By starting with what you want/need to make and work that number back, you are breaking it down to daily, weekly, or monthly goals.

For Example:

If I want to gross $100,000:

$100,000 / 250 days = $400 divide into 5

(number of average guests per day I have)

My average service ticket will be $80!

(This is before taxes, and you can decide if this is with or without tips.)

If you are on commission, take your commission percentage rate times your desired gross number—that will give you your gross after commission.

By walking into the salon in the morning and saying, "Today I NEED each of my guest's average service ticket to be $80," do you think I am more likely to hit that number than if I walk in and say, "Well, I hope today is good."?

This is where I have to go.

These are the steps I have to take.

This is how I get there.

Walk those steps.

And you will get there!

What is considered a FULL BOOK?

Alright, this calls for some math!

How many clients do we need to have a full book?

- **1 client per hour**
- **8 working hours in a day**
- **22 working days in a month**
- **176 clients per month**
- **x 12 months per year**
- **2,112 client visits per year**
- **Now we need to figure the Frequency of Visit or the FOV**
- **On average, a client visits every 6 weeks**
- **52 weeks in year**
- **That's 8 times a year**
- **2,112 divided by 8 = 254 clients for a full book**

Now that's if you want one guest per hour. Think haircut only. Let's take it a step further by thinking smarter not harder.

- **1 client every 3 hours**
- **3 clients in a day**
- **66 clients per month x 12 = 792 visits per year**
- **Divide by 8 = 99**

I only need 99 ride-or-die color clients to have a full book making $100,000 (that's without tips and retail commission)! Can we say HAIR BOSS?

STOP! JUST STOP!! See what I mean when I say if we have a map we know how to get to our desired destination!?

What's the best way to fine tune that book?

Once you have an average of 99 color guests per month plus all of your non-color guests, you can fine-tune them. Phase out the lower paying guests. Yeah, I know we worked hard to get to this point. Why would we want to phase out or give away a guest? Because doing so will open your book to someone that can be filled with a color. Or if you'd like to keep the lower ticket guests, offer them time in the hours that are slower. High-paying guests get the prime-time spots on your books.

How do I cross-promote in a salon?

Network with massage and nails. Run promotions with them. Mani and blowout special with Jamie and Alyssa for only $39.

Bridal party comes in for nails, you hand out cards.

Massage guest comes in, let him know at the front that you will touch up his hair after his massage for a complimentary service. I like to call these planting seeds. You are creating relationships, introducing yourself, and the guests will be more likely to return because they already know you!

If there is a makeup artist in house, ask if she would give complimentary touchups to your guest's hairline after their color service. Also, lipstick touchups. She can cross-promote with your guests, and they leave happy knowing they look well put together.

Running effective promotions

**Fresh, new, out-of-school promotion –
Complimentary haircut with color service**

New guest promotion – $25 gift for first service

**Returning guest promotion – After a first visit,
receive a thank you gift of a gift card for a complimentary deep condition treatment on next visit**

Referral programs – $10, $15, or $20 for referrals

**Loyalty promotion – (Can be based on how much
they spend or how many times they come in.
Retention is huge, and these promotions offer our
loyal guests a thank you.)**

What's the best way to create a promotion?

There is a smart way to market! It is important how we say things when offering promotions. The wording of a promotion can make or break its outcome. It comes down to communication. For example, consider the difference in how the following are worded. How do you think each would be received by a guest? Does one offer feel better to a guest? Does one offer change the client's per-ception of your value?

$25 *Gift* toward your next service

versus

$25 off your next service

How do I get word-of-mouth traffic in my chair?

Ask! The best way to get word-of-mouth traffic is to ask your current guests to brag about you.

Here is an easy script to write down and memorize.

"In the next 24-48 hours, you are going to get so many compliments on your hair, and when you do can you please give them this referral card (or business card) because I want more people like you in my chair!"

Ask what your guest is doing that day or week and who is she going to see.

When she says, "I'm going to lunch with my friend Naomi today!" write out a $20 gift card addressed to Naomi and have your client share it with her friend. This technique is effective, and the guest is excited to give her friend something of value such as a referral to a new hairdresser!

How do I set my limits with family/friends on discounting and working at home?

By saying NO and setting a limit. For myself, I do my children and my husband at home and that's all. After that, you are considered my guest and must come to the salon to see me.

Otherwise it's like a doctor doing full workups in his kitchen. He wouldn't do that for his cousin or neighbor. It's weird, not to mention illegal.

Why do I want to volunteer my time?

Our craft is one of the most beautiful things to volunteer and offer as a help in some way. We make people feel beautiful about themselves. The first time I volunteered at a woman's shelter changed my life. Giving haircuts to a mom and her three small children impacted them and me. They were so grateful. She said they hadn't had anything positive in so long that the hairstyles meant the world to them. She said they never know where they will get their next meal or where they will sleep. She said getting something as simple as a haircut from someone who cares was life changing.

Something I learned a long time ago from one of my mentors, Chris Baran. The more you give away, the more good comes to you. Those words have impacted my life tremendously. The more we give away, the more comes to us. Wow.

As powerful as this fact is, it can be difficult to believe. Often, we find that if something good comes to us, we like to keep it that way; if it's good it's ours and no one else can have it. This could be true about our occupation, money, love, generosity, etc.

However, the moment you open yourself up and allow others to have what you have, or to share what you know, or give what you can offer . . . you find that this act of helping others takes your life to the next level. We make a difference. So, I challenge you to volunteer your craft. And see what happens in return. Here is a list of ideas.

- **One Mission Buzz for Kids** – Volunteer opportunities to shave heads of those who have raised money for children fighting cancer.
- **Women's shelters**
- **Ronald McDonald House** – Offer your services to the families of children in the hospital fighting for their lives.

- **VA hospitals** – Offer your services to those who served this country.

- **Local shelters** – Contact your local shelter to see if you can offer your services to those staying at the shelter. Go as a team or a with a few fellow hairdressers to make a greater impact on the shelter and on those men, women, and children in need of something as simple and as important as a haircut.

Retail Versus Recommend

What is retail?

The retail portion in cosmetology school is definitely a swift kick in the butt. This is the moment when you realize you didn't come to school to just learn how to style hair. You discover that you need to sell along with doing hair. It was toward the middle of my schooling that I remember getting extremely upset about retail. I didn't want to sell; I wanted to do hair. Being a pushy salesperson by showing a cream to a client just to make my numbers was not appealing. In fact, I remained bitterly stubborn against retail for the first few years of my career because I didn't have the proper guidance to understand exactly what the role of retail in our industry actually is.

So here it is . . . the truth. The real face of retail in the beauty industry. Which took me years to understand, learn, and then master. So, if you're reading this and you're new to the industry, I feel like I'm handing down imperative knowledge that may save you years of learning the hard way.

When you think of retail what do you think? If you're like most people, you think:

- **Sales**
- **Money**
- **Commission**
- **Pushy**

As hairdressers, we are the complete opposite of these words. We are caring and nurturing by nature. Selling isn't why we entered this profession. It's not what we are about. So, retail is difficult for us! And that's okay!

Here's the good news, though at first it may look like bad news. The news: We have been lied to for many years. About this big R word. We ask each other what our retail to service percentage is etc. We talk about retail and how much we have sold in a month. But this entire time, the R word is not in fact Retail. The true R word is Recommend. What is our recommendation to service percentage? What are we recommending to our guests so that they can achieve the style they want on their own?

When you think of the word *recommend*, what comes to mind?

- **Expertise**
- **Professional**
- **Advice**
- **Knowledgeable**
- **Trusting**

Now think of the first person you call when you need a recommendation. Who is it? Usually it's your mom or dad, best friend, husband, wife. Someone that you TRUST. Someone that you know is an expert or is very knowledgeable in life to help you with a solid opinion.

Our guests do that with us. They need someone to help them, and who better than us to guide them? Once we have gained their trust, they ask for our recommendations. Whether we notice the question or not, they are asking us. Think about how we do this with other professionals we need an opinion from. Like our doctor. We go to our doctor when we have an ailment because we have a desire or a need that has to be met. Our doctor then comes up with the cause of our ailment and writes us a prescription to help or cure our ailment or issue. We take that prescription to the pharmacy, and when our pharmacist tells us our insurance isn't going to cover the bill, what do we do? We huff a little under our breath, but we pay the bill because this is what the expert told us we need for the issue. The issue is why we go to see a doctor in the first place. We trust their opinion and know that when we use what they recommended it will help us with our issue.

When we change our perspective from retail to recommendation, that is when we are truly understanding our role and can embrace it and be willing to help our guest in every way possible.

It's not about selling them products.

It's about offering SOLUTIONS to our clients' wants, desires, and needs.

Let me say this again . . . it's not about selling, it's about solutions.

They ask for your help, and you recommend a technique on how to style their hair, or a product to tame their frizz. You can suggest a tool they can use to create that wave or dry the hair smooth.

You can offer the solution for their problem that they expect to receive from you—your professional advice.

Our industry has shied away from the professionalism inherent in our business. Not on purpose, of course. We have shied away from the professional stance because we get to know our guests on an intimate level. We are one of the few professions that get to touch another human being, but in a good way. The guest looks forward to this appointment. When was the last time you thought, "Oh yes, I can't wait to go to the dentist!"? But our guests are excited to see us. Many can't wait to get their hair done. And so those lines of professionalism and intimacy get blurred. Some become close to us, almost like family, especially after many years of doing their hair. If we can keep just enough of that professionalism, and incorporate it into the relationship, we have a strong bond of trust. When they come to us with a problem, we should recommend a solution that they can act on with trust and confidence in our advice. Then the guest is happy, and we are happy that they are able to achieve their goals.

When do you recommend?

Recommending a product has somehow evolved to a point where this activity is performed at the end of a visit. When the client is going to the front to pay for the service and get ready to leave.

In reality, this is the WORST time to introduce and recommend a product. Once you pop the collar on the cape, consider the client already out the door. Their minds are onto other things, such as, where are my keys, how much is this again, do I have food at home for dinner or should I stop, I think I need to fuel the car, etc. They have already mentally checked out from you and this experience.

This is how it should be done: 90 percent of our recommendations should happen during the consultation, 5 percent at the shampoo bowl or during the service, and 5 percent when finishing and educating them on how to style their own hair at home. No recommendations should be given in the reception area at the end (unless they ask for it, of course).

I've included some helpful examples!

Consultation

The client tells you about her issues, wants, desires, needs, etc. You repeat back to her (for example), "So, what I'm hearing is that you are struggling with frizz on a daily basis. I'm going to recommend _____product. When you use this, you will no longer have frizz. I will show you how to use it when we get to the haircut and finish."

Shampoo Experience

The shampoo experience is the most critical moment in the entire appointment. This is where 70 percent of our guests will decide if they are coming back to us or not. So, when they ask what you are using or proclaim how amazing the smell is, this is your opportunity to talk about the shampoo you're using. Hit them with the benefits. Don't go deep into the ingredients; that can be too much. Focus on how it will help them at home. "This is by Pureology, and it's their moisture shampoo, which I chose for you because I noticed your hair was dry. Just wait until you see the results when we blow-dry!"

Color Service

Again, speak to the benefits of pre-treatments, glazes, a chem-
ical bonder such as olaplex or ph bonder. Briefly explain the reasons why you are recommending this exact product for them during
their color services.

Haircut/Styling

This is when you get to educate them on the recommendations
you gave them during the consultation. Really concentrate on
education. Since we are around hair all the time, we think everyone knows just as much as we do about hair. In fact, most clients
don't. They really look to us as the experts who can help them.
Show them exactly what you are doing. How you are applying, and
where you are applying. Approach this as if you are teaching how
to do what you do, and pretend they are blind. "I put two pumps
of the smoothing lotion in my hand and work it around, then I apply
to the densest part of your hair first and then work forward." Don't
assume they can follow what you're doing solely with their eyes.
Explain it to them in detail with your words. Same with styling, tell
them how to use the brush and blow-dryer. And when finishing the
hair, show them how to curl or flat iron. If they want to learn how to
braid, show them that. All of this will prove to your guest that you
are attentive and you care about her.

HAIR BOSS HACK: Here is the formula for recommending.

If you have _____ (issue or desire)

Then I recommend _____ (product)

When you use that, you will no longer have

_____ (emphasize the solution).

So here goes . . .

If you have frizz, then I recommend Pureology Smooth Perfection Shampoo and Condition. When you use that, you will no longer struggle with frizz.

If you want volume in your style, I recommend Clean Volume Levitation Mist. When you use that, you will get the lift and hold that you are looking for.

How do I teach my client at-home care?

At-home care is one of the largest aspects of client service we skip over when assisting our guests on a daily basis. How often do we hear them say, "Oh, I wish I could just take you home with me and you could do my hair every day!" If you need a BIG SIGN that your guest is ASKING you for at-home care, it is in this moment! They want you to come home with them! Then you say, "Well, guess what? You can! I'll give you my day rate and mileage fee at the end of the visit. . . . Ha-ha. No, seriously though, you can. I will teach you to do what I do and use what I use. Then you can do this at home just the way I do it here."

USE WHAT I USE

DO WHAT I DO

Social Media Exposure

What's the best way to use social media to catapult my career?

Social media is the single most disruptive marketing tool in two decades. The world has never seen anything like this, and it's only evolving at lightning speed. We have seen social media transform average hairdressers to the face of beauty products. Social media has a direct effect on the color and products being developed and used regularly in salons. It drives trends. What an amazing time in our hairdressing lives! If you put in the work, you can directly affect the trends that are happening in our culture. You can become a brand yourself, and people will come from miles away to see you.

Knowing which social platform is the right fit for you is a start. Facebook acts more like a newspaper. It highlights our birthdays and anniversaries, funnies, and memes. It is also a great platform for videos and live feeds. The average user of Facebook is 45- to 65-year-old women. Do we have those women in our chairs? YES, and if that is your ideal client, then Facebook is where you will want to put the majority of your time.

Instagram is more like a magazine. Which is great because we are a visual industry. Our art is visual. Showcasing a visual to the masses is the easiest way to gain new guests via social media. The majority of Instagram users are between 17 to 35 years old.

So, finding your ideal guest is priority. Then go after them where they are! My focus is Instagram as that is where my ideal guests show up daily, and so that's the majority of information I will be offering to you.

How to get exposure and gain new clients?

Social media is the single fastest way to build your book at an alarming rate. It all comes down to how much time and effort you put into it. How much you want to get out of it is how much you should put into it. Even allowing 15 minutes a day dedicated to business building via social media amounts to 105 minutes a week and 7 hours a month. Start small, then build from there. We spend an average of three hours a day on our phones: 87 percent of that time is spent on mobile apps. Wouldn't it make sense to use that time with PURPOSE? Use your time on your phone in such a way that it will directly affect your income and livelihood.

One of the most amazing aspects of social media is local influencers in your area. Even if you aren't located in a large city, I promise you they are everywhere! Just by researching on Instagram, you will be able to find social influencers.

HAIR BOSS HACK: Offer social influencers weekly blow-outs in exchange for shout-outs on their page. You want to offer them something in return for a few minutes of their social platform. They have leverage within your city and region of what's cool and happening. Having them in your chair will give you exposure to your ideal clients in your target market.

How can I gain new clients by creating content?

Create content in the salon by taking photos of your guest's hair. Make sure you ask for their permission to photograph them and feature them on your page. This sounds better than, "Can I take a picture of you?" Be sure to tag them in your photo when you post it. This will open up your reach to their followers.

Feature clients weekly or daily if you can. Utilize Instagram stories as well.

Something that I have done successfully is to add on 10 minutes to my bookings so that I have time to take a photo at the end. Remember, this is advertising for your business. Treat it like it matters, because it does. Keep in mind that there is a return on your investment in taking the time to take pictures to post later. Learn how to take a good photo, and make each photo as beautiful as you can.

Why less is more in quality of photos?

Social media is ever changing. So, if I were to tell you what is happening right now in trends, by the time you read this something else will be new! That's how quickly it changes. Instead, focus on less is more. Avoid taking photos of your guests while they are sitting in your chair. Have them go outside or stand against a blank wall. If you have a fancy camera phone, you can take it anywhere and blur the background. Think less is more.

When posting, be selective. A few of something good is better than a lot of bad photos. You want it to be aesthetically pleasing to the eye.

Instagram is a visual platform. Think of it as your own personal magazine of your work and business. Ask yourself, "Would I put this in a magazine?" If the answer is no, then don't post it.

What's the best way to target the 45- to 65-year-old demographic?

This age demographic is participating more on Facebook than on any other platform. If you are targeting these guests, this is where you will find them.

Utilizing Facebook's business page will increase your exposure to potential guests. It has a number of benefits such as building brand loyalty, and increasing your web traffic. It can reach a targeted audience and gather leads. It is also one of the lowest marketing expenses out there. You can utilize the insights to gather info on which promos do well and which don't. And finally, it has Facebook Messenger. This is a direct line to potential future guests. You can send them a promo or link to your site to book with you through Messenger.

What's the best way to target the 18- to 35-year-old demographic?

This age demographic is primarily on Instagram. Yet that number is expanding. The number one fastest user joining is a 38-year-old. If you are targeting this age group for your ideal client, then you will want to utilize Instagram.

Instagram also has Instastories, which allows us to connect quickly with our followers. This is a great way to show how fun and exciting you and your salon are.

Instagram's DM feature is the money piece. This is how and where you will build your career. It gives you access to direct message potential clients, influencers, and anyone who has an account on IG. I will say that some of my greatest opportunities to date have come from Instagram DM.

How can I create credibility?

In our world, having credibility is half the battle, whether it's with our guests or other professionals. A sure way to gain instant credibility is by creating a website. The website need not be complicated. It can be a simple page that provides a snapshot of your business or name, a location of where you can be reached, where your salon is, photos of your work, and photos of you doing hair. When you are promoting yourself, you can say, "Check out my work at www.jamiewiley.com" and they have a clickable link straight to you and your brand.

HAIR BOSS HACK: Include a direct link to your online booking system on your website, so when they check out your work, they can book with you immediately!

Credibility can also come from a publication. Maybe your local newspaper can run a story or feature you. (All you have to do is ask.) When you have a publication, you gain credibility.

Testimonials are another avenue of credibility. Ask your current guests for testimonials to publish online. They give you credibility. Also, a positive review is 500 percent better than any paid advertisement! Focus on this one.

How can I see new trends?

Subscribe to hair publications such as *Modernsalon, American Salon, Hairbrained, Bangstyle* to name a few.

Research history . . . it truly does repeat itself! When things are long, next season they will be short. When it's out, then it will be in. If it's straight, then it will be curly. When you watch the trends, you can see how they sway and flow and repeat in cycles. This will give you an edge and know what to expect. But there are some trends we hope that will never see the light of day again. Ha!

Alright. Let's talk about the love–hate relationship we have with Pinterest. We love to look at it for inspiration, but we hate it when our guests go overboard with it. What is so exciting about Pinterest is that *we*, as in hairdressers, are posting photos and setting trends. The average hairdresser is creating what is coming and going in our industry, and that's exciting! It used to be that our guests would wait until a celebrity had a hairstyle or color before they thought it's okay to do it. But now our guest will see it on Pinterest and jump right in! Clients will often show you photos from other hairdressers that they found on Pinterest. We have the POWER to create trends and to showcase on Instagram or Pinterest, and then another woman will find that photo and bring it to her hairdresser.

How can I learn new products?

Social media is the perfect place to see the newest and hottest products. It's also a place to see what is coming. Often times brands will tease their new products launching soon. This is the only place to get a sneak peek!

What the celebrities are using, our guests will be using as soon as they see it on social media. From top educators in the industry to celebrities, those are the products that perform and get the most buzz on social media.

How can I be featured . . . what are the best practices?

Tag. Tag. Tag. On social media, you want to have a large reach, and the way to get that is to tag your photo. Who should you tag?

- Brand of tools that you are using
- Professional brands that you are using
- Distributors
- Magazines and hair pages

Perfect your work and watch other professionals that you are inspired by. If they are getting features, recreate what they are doing.

What's the best way to land a local blogger/high-profile guest?

Instagram! Network on Instagram. It is the new way of con-necting and networking. Use the direct message feature. Offer something of value first, then pitch how you'd like to cross-promote.

Tell her that you would love to give her a complimentary blowout before the next event she has. Once you get to know her, she will start shouting you out on her Instagram that has 60K followers. That's free advertising to locals! Do not underestimate the power of an amazing blowout!

How can I go viral on the internet?

You can't go viral unless you have content. Create content first, get in the game, then go live with it! Once it's up, post in more than one location. Ask your followers to like, comment, and share. Don't be afraid to share with other professionals on hair forums. Ask for involvement! The more engagement, the longer it will stay live and gain more views. If you need to tag your friends and family to get it started, then do so! And don't be afraid of the promote button! This is a great way to get in front of your target audience.

How can I get my work published?

Session work requires a team. Find a team! Get creative and let your inner child come out to play. Remember when we were little and all that we had to worry about was playing and creating. There was no right or wrong answer; it just came from within. Tap back into that creative space. Play with hair. Think back to the last time that you put on some music and played with hair. This is one of my favorite activities. I often will include my daughters and ask if they want to play with me with my dolls! This allows your passion and creativity to emerge. You will surprise yourself!

Shoot your collection or ideas with your team and a model. Have the photographer edit the photos and submit to magazines online. There are hundreds of magazines that are looking for YOUR content. If you get a rejection, move on to the next publication. Remember, N.O. really means "next opportunity"! Getting 10 NO's before for the 1 YES is fine! All you need is that one yes.

What's the best way to write a press release?

A press release is an official announcement issued to the news media. The heading should contain action verbs, the first paragraph should answer the main questions of who, what, why, and where. The press release should contain understandable language and a quote of some kind. It's more about providing relevant content when and how your prospects, influencers, and customers will consume it.

Best practices when writing a press release include: making your headline irresistible. Tell them why they should care; this is where you put your who, what, why, where, and how of your launch or development. Bring it to life by using an eye-catching quote. Quoting key figures or authorities underlines the importance of your press release.

There are no cut-and-dry rules when it comes to press releases, but here are a few reasons why it's good to do one—opening a new location, introducing a new partner, rebranding, promoting/hiring a new executive, and receiving an award.

You'll want to submit locally first then take it nationally. Tip: sending it to a specific writer rather than the entire publication may get your foot in the door faster.

PRESS RELEASE EXAMPLE

replace with
LOGO

Contact Jamie Wiley
Telephone [Company Phone]
Cell [Cell Phone]
Email [Company E-mail]
Website [Website]

FOR IMMEDIATE RELEASE
[Date]

[MAIN TITLE OF PRESS RELEASE IN ALL CAPS]

[Subtitle of Press Release]

[City], [ST], [Date]– [Insert your announcement here and then briefly describe the benefits.]

[Insert a quote from a company executive about what the announcement means.]

[Add additional paragraph(s) as necessary to describe your announcement and the benefits it provides.]

[Insert a customer quote or news about partnering with another company, if appropriate.]

[Insert your company's boilerplate message.]

# # #

If you would like more information about this topic, please contact Jamie Wiley at [Company Phone] or email at [Company E-mail].

Networking

How to start networking before you need it.

Our world is one big network. Meeting and networking with as many people as possible will create long-lasting relationships and collaborations. When networking, remember that everyone has equal value. From a high-profile artist, all the way down to the artist that is newer in the industry, each and every person you meet has the potential to grow your career. You never know what each person or opportunity will present to you. Some of the most amazing experiences happened from networking with similarly skilled creative professionals. The connections that they had and offered me pushed me further in my career.

Do your research when looking to network. What event or hair show are you attending? Find out about the artists who will be attending, and prepare to network with them.

When networking, you want to look for gain:

- Gaining referrals
- Gaining exposure
- Gaining opportunities to grow
- Gaining experience
- Gaining mentorship

As you advance in your career, so does the networking.

Go big. When you gain more experience and exposure, so should your networking. Ask 100 times, get let down 99. Check back in with them if they gave you a NO. Circle back a year later. You also want to give before you can expect to get. Think about offering your assistance in exchange for collaborations, a mentorship, etc.

Think about different avenues in networking as well. Maybe it was someone you met years ago that you could reconnect with. Or visit LinkedIn to do research on potential networking opportunities. Make connections now that may help you later on in your career. You never know who or when they will circle back around. That initial connection could make or break your career. Connect sooner rather than later.

Remember, networking isn't about taking. It's about giving first; then receiving something in return. Networking is a reciprocal activity. If you focus on the return, then you will come across as inauthentic and only in it for yourself. Networking is a two-way connection. Plant the seeds, water them, and let them grow. And one day you will have a beautiful forest of opportunities all from making connections throughout your journey.

Editorial Styling And Traveling

Would you like to be a part of fashion week?

Yes, but how?! It's a BIG feat to add to your resume. Fashion week usually appears on the bucket list of many hairdressers. You will want to gain experience first. Large cities have fashion week. Find the designers and artists that are keying the shows, and ask if you can assist. This is your first step. You can also call local agencies and ask to assist their hair artists.

This area of the industry is where you will have to volunteer your time before getting paid to do this trade. Volunteering is a great way to gain experience and the particular skill set needed. Usually the hairdressers that get paid for fashion week are those that are keying the show. Once you gain experience and exposure, you can work your way up to bigger cities and bigger designers.

Instagram and Facebook are another way to seek those hairdressers who need support during fashion week. Make yourself available to them. Fashion week shows, keys, and artists are finalized in the last few weeks, days, and hours leading up to the show. Being flexible will give you a leg up.

How can I inspire other professionals at hair trade shows?

Be a part of a brand so that you can showcase your work and talent at industry hair shows. Aligning and training with a brand will get you to the stage at hair shows. Being with a brand allows you to represent something bigger than yourself, as well as learning new and cutting-edge techniques. You can then share those techniques with hundreds and maybe even thousands of hair professionals. In this unique and important way, you are truly gaining advanced education and then giving it to the hairdressers that come to see you. It is one of the most amazing experiences.

It will rejuvenate and inspire you personally as well as professionally. Being a part of something bigger than you, and of something that you love, always launches you into the stratosphere. Make hair shows a priority.

What is freelance work?

Freelance is any kind of work that comes directly to you with no middle man. You choose if you want to accept the job or pass. This kind of work can be finicky. It is not always consistent, especially when you are first starting out. The upside is that it can be very satisfying when you land gigs that are high paying.

You also can do your own advertising and search for work on your own. Use Instagram as a way to showcase your book and advertise to potential freelance job opportunities. Apply to be a part of an agency that will then bring work to you.

The best way to build a freelance book is by connecting with a makeup artist. When he receives a gig, he can recommend you. And vice versa.

Some hair artists connect with local photographers. They are also working on building a portfolio and need someone like you to provide your expertise. Recommendations can flow both ways when you find a photographer you enjoy working with.

Another way is by offering to assist local freelance artists that are doing well. That way, you can make connections and learn at the same time. And eventually when that hair artist is sick or passes on a job, she will ask you.

How do I find a team to work with?

This can be a difficult challenge, finding a team that allows you to be creative and who is supportive at the same time. Instagram is a great place to start your search! There are other sites, such as model mayhem, that can give you access to photographers, makeup artists, and models. Shoot with a few photographers and makeup artists and when you find the people you enjoy and connect with, keep shooting and producing. You will push each other and make each other better.

What does editorial mean?

Editorial hair or fashion is something that would be shown in a magazine. It usually has a storyline and a number of different looks or even multiple models. There are less rules in this category.

What does advertising mean?

This is when a company is selling a product or brand. Advertising tends to look cleaner with simple lighting to really show off the clothing or makeup. Editorial and advertising often get confused. Editorial sells a mood, while advertising sells a thing.

What does high fashion mean?

Haute couture is French for "high dressmaking" or "high fashion." This term is thrown around loosely in our industry. It's a step up from fashion and a step below couture. It can be vague, but that is part of its appeal. Think of high fashion as bold statements and luxury.

What's the best way to get into the wedding world?

Weddings can be one of the best ways to create a substantial earning. There are professionals who will only do weddings and can make a month's salary in a weekend. Brides are more than ever searching for a hairdresser to fit her particular wants and needs. One of those needs may be on-site services. She is looking to book an artist that will come to her. Working in an environment such as a wedding party on the day of a wedding, on site, is exciting and fun! Being a part of a woman's special day and working in that energy is exhilarating!

DO'S AND DONT'S

- **DO:** Assist, find a mentor that you can assist and learn the ins and outs of hairdressing from for formal occasions. A mentor will show you how to set up, what to bring, and what products and tools you must have in your kit.

- **DO**: Write up a contract for ALL of your brides and bridal parties. Have them make a down payment to reserve that date with you. And collect the remaining fee on the day of.

- **DO**: Advertise yourself with local wedding dress shops, venue locations, and wedding photographers. You may even offer a bundle package with any of these professionals.

- **DON'T**: Overbook yourself. Two weddings in one day is tough. You never know what might happen at the first location that will set your time off. Then showing up to the next location late will give you bad review, one that you may never rise above.

What does on-site work mean?

On-site means any paid work that you perform outside of the salon or your place of business. This is when someone is asking you to perform your skill at a certain location.

When working on-site, be sure to ask about a power source for your irons or blow-dryer.

Also keep in mind how you will be charging for your services. Writing up an invoice and sending it over beforehand for review and approval in writing is imperative.

INVOICE EXAMPLE

HAIR BOSS

INVOICE

555-123-4567
EMAIL ADDRESS
WEBSITE

ADDRESS
CITY, STATE

Attention: NAME OF BUSINESS OR PERSON RECEIVING SERVICES
THEIR ADDRESS
CITY, STATE
DATE:

Project Title:
Invoice Number:
Terms: (NUMBER OF DAYS/HOURS)

Description	Quantity	Unit Price	Cost
ON SITE HAIR - MOVIE SET	1	$ 1,000	$ 1,000
AIRFARE	1	$ 250	$ 250
DEPOSIT		$ 0	$ 0
		Subtotal	$ 1,250
	Tax	0.00%	$ 0
		Total	$ 1,250

Thank you for the selection. I appreciate the business and look forward to working with you and your team!

See you soon

Respectfully,

Jamie Wiley

How do I break into the movie and TV session world?

Assisting is the quickest way to break into the world of movie and television. Every city has television stations that you can do hair for before their people go on-screen. Movies are another beast all together. You may need to live in or travel to larger cities that host movie production companies.

Look for casting calls for talent and models. Research who will be the key hairstylist. Then reach out to them!

Be aware that movie set life is long and wearing. This is an avenue that is rewarding, but also can be grueling because of the demanding hours. Movie productions will shoot at all hours of the day and days of the week. Committing to a movie is exciting, but also a huge commitment. Making sure that you have adequate child care or support in your life to make this happen is crucial!

Financial Freedom

What does financial freedom look like to you?

Financial freedom looks different for everyone. Making millions can mean financial freedom for some. While making ends meet and fulfilling a budget is financial freedom to others. Finding what it means to you is what's important. One thing I like to do at the start of every year is make a list. It looks like this.

If there was no way to fail...

In six months:

I would HAVE-

I would BE-

I would DO-

And in twelve months:

I would HAVE-

I would BE-

I would DO-

Write out a list from a place of no limits. Do not put a cap on the possibility of the things that are the most sacred in your soul. The exercise of dreaming goals is liberating. It is also a powerful means of manifestation. If we have the courage to speak it to the universe, even if only in a whisper, we have the courage to see it come to pass.

How do I achieve financial freedom?

The old mind-set was that we have to work till we are 65, then we retire. The prime of our life is 25 to 65. Go where you want to go, and do what you want to do, when you want to do it.

Even when you start a family. This is often the time when society says we should settle, and wait till our kids are older to continue our own journey. But what does that teach our children?

I worked 40 hours a week in a commission salon when I had a toddler and baby at home. My husband worked Monday through Friday 9 to 5, and so I worked 40 hours a week during nights and weekends. That meant we never saw each other, and I never saw him with my kids at the same time. We were passing ships in the night. After living like that for two years, I knew I never wanted to do that again. Figuring it out the hard way almost cost me my career. It was something that I loved and was so passionate about, but I was putting it ahead of the ones that I hold most dear to me and without them none of it is worth it. So, I stepped back and said

STOP! I don't like this. I want my career and passion, but I want my financial freedom to do it when I want to do it.

I figured out how many guests I would need to sustain my FF and how much average service ticket I would need in order to achieve it. I wanted to cut my days down from 6 days a week working the worst shifts to 3 days working the best shifts. I did it gradually. Going to 5 then 4 then 3 in a matter of 8 months. Once I was at 3 days a week I worked 6 to 10 hour days. Depending on the day. Plus, I used the formula of 99 ride or die color clients given to you earlier to achieve financial freedom!

Financial freedom is attainable. Envision it for yourself. Plan it out. Then work toward it.

This book will give you the heads up. It has years of industry secrets that took me a long time to learn and also earn. I am grateful for those who have shared their wisdom gained through experience with me, and now I am passing them on to you. Because I want nothing more than to see us all succeed. I believe there is room enough in this big, beautiful world for all of us who want to flourish and to reach the place in our life that feels and looks good. I would like to help you get there, so we can all enjoy it to the fullest, and then help others who come after us.

The Road To Success

How can I place my passion first and income second?

Focus on what you love. Think of the reason behind you becom-ing a hairdresser in the first place. Write it down so that you remember it during the difficult times. Actually, go ahead and write it here.

MY REASON. MY WHY.

When our WHY becomes greater than everything else, that is when we push to greatness. It gives our life meaning and a higher purpose. When that happens, we can do amazing things.

Where we conduct our passion is vital if we are to flourish as human beings. Our career makes up 1/3 of our life, so spending it at a salon or location that makes you angry, sad, or depressed isn't worth it. Focus on what makes you truly happy.

Are you happy and in love with your current situation? If the answer is no, then I will be the higher voice in this moment that says it shouldn't be like that. You already know it deep down. Make the change to move on. After all, it is your precious life and you only get one shot at it. Make it count. Don't wait.

Drama, negativity, and disrespect are all things we should stay away from. It affects our mental health, self-esteem, and longevity in this career. The breakroom can be an area where this kind of negativity happens. This is where careers go to die. Stay away. Stay busy. The bottom 80 percent live in the breakroom.

Income will follow when your passion comes first. In the beginning, Steve Jobs endured years of ridicule and had to endure thousands of nay-sayers. He pushed through because he was passionate. He had a vision, and he put himself in the future and could see it even when no one else could. And look at where the world is now because of his endurance.

Who is the top 20 percent?

Top earners in our industry are often times referred to as the top 20 percent. These are the hairstylists that track their numbers, promote themselves, take continuing education seriously and consistently, and hustle every day. They are HAIR BOSSES.

They get to this position because of the hard work and dedication they have committed to themselves and their craft. They are focused, and they document their numbers every day, week, and month. They want to see their growth and know when they are slacking. There are amazing companies such as Summit Salon that assist stylists and salons in evaluating and elevating themselves.

An industry mentor that has a vast range of knowledge is Michael Cole. If you aren't following him already, begin now. He shares how to maximize your books and also highlights hairstylists that are doing amazing work in the field.

Business Knowledge

This is where you can crunch the numbers to see where you stand in the hair game.

- **Average service ticket –** This is what your guests are spending on average. How to find this figure is total service sales divided by the number of clients serviced. That will equal your average service ticket.

- **Client retention –** This when a client returns to you and the salon. Having a high client retention means higher average tickets. They will then buy more from you on subsequent visits, and they will recommend you to others.

- **Retail to service percent -** Take your service ticket for the day and divide that by your retail sold and that gives you your retail to service percent.

The average retail to service is 8 percent. Which is not good. Living around the 20 percent RTS is ideal. If you aren't there or near there, you know you have work to do. If you're at or over 20 percent, congrats! You are rocking it!

Here We Go, Hair Boss

The last nine chapters are now sitting at your fingertips, ready for a refresh whenever you need or want it. It is up to you what you do with the instructions presented here. Remember, one step at a time is how we dance, and it will happen for you if you take the time to learn the steps, practice them, and practice them some more. More than anything, remember how fun it is to dance, and enjoy it to the fullest.

MOTIVATION

It all comes down to motivation. Because ultimately, we live our lives in cages, but the door to that cage is wide open. It is up to us to fly free. Motivation will push your why. And your WHY is something that is bigger than your excuses.

Those excuses are the little voices in our head. I like to call this place the MATRIX. It's the space that we believe is our reality; we tell ourselves false information to keep us feeling safe in our comfort zone. The comfort zone of our cage.

These voices tell us we aren't good enough...

We are too old...

Too young...

Not talented enough...

Don't have enough experience...

We are overweight...

We are not smart enough . . .

The list goes on...

Even now as I write this I'm working through the negativity of my little voices. They are always there. But we are stronger than they are. We can condition our brains to shut down the little voices. They will always be there but we can ignore them and push on.

FEAR

Do we have fear, or does fear have us? There is a big differ-ence. Fear can imprison us. It can keep us from true happiness. It can keep us from adventure. Excitement. Travel. We give permission to fear to keep us in that frozen state of mind. This is the MATRIX; succumbing to the little voices and fear. Acknowledge it. Then turn it off.

Life is about growth. Find someone that you can GROW with and who will move you forward and face fears together over and over again. Someone that will push you. Someone who won't let you off the hook. Someone who will hold you to the fire because they know you will be stronger because of it.

If we succumb to those voices, we remained locked in our safe zone. But in that safe zone, we will never grow. We will stagnate. And when we are 89 looking back on our lives, we will feel the pain of regret. So, you can face the pain of going outside of your comfort zone now and live the life you imagined. Or live with the pain of regret later on. Either way it's going to be painful. Choose which one you'd rather feel.

GIVING UP

The biggest lesson I have learned in this industry is this. There will be a lot of down moments. Moments that make you want to give up. Throw in the towel. Switch careers. Clients can be rude. Fellow hairdressers can be cruel. During those down moments, remember that you must go through those times to give you the thick skin necessary for the long haul.

Those down moments are where growth takes place. This is when you will be shaped into the hairdresser that you will become for the rest of your career. And sometimes in those down moments you find your voice. You find your swing, and you learn how to hit back.

Instead of giving up, recycle your pain. Take that pain and let it drive you forward.

Make progress. It will give you happiness and move you along this journey.

It is not about what happens to you. Life is about what you do AFTER it happens to you. How will you react? Because 20 percent of people don't care about your problems, and the other 80 percent are happy that you have them. So, knowing this, moving forward learn to rely on yourself and not others.

CHOICES

You chose this profession for a reason. It was seeking you just as much as you were seeking it. And now you are on your way to a greater life by enhancing the lives of others. Leading a fulfilling life will give you more purpose than one that was forced down your throat. Earl Nightingale once said,

"We become what we think about."

Imagine that. You become what you think about. Our thoughts control our life. If you focus on positive things, positive things happen. If you focus on the negative, then negative things happen. Focus on your strengths. And do more of that. Do more of the positive things you see and want for your life.

FOCUS

Manage your time. Control the first hour of your day or the last hour of your day. Make those 60 minutes for you and your personal growth.

After a certain amount of focused effort, we struggle from mental fatigue. So, take breaks but don't be quiet forever.

When you write your goals down, you start to see the answers around you. You start to see the opportunities that align with your goal. Your brain is a magnet, and it will find the answers for you. Because you put yourself out there and you are conscious about it now.

CREATIVITY

The human learns best by pulling the information in, not push-ing it. The brain works through creation not consumption.

So, when you want to create and innovate, take away the technology and you will find that your mind will wander with wonder and you are able to create. Just like when we were kids. This is called white space. Take time for it. Go for walks, breathe, meditate, play. We need white space in our lives to innovate and reconnect with our souls. Connect with that place of creativity. You don't need to think about judgment or opinions. Just create and play and pretend the sky is the limit. Let your creativity come from inside you.

SUMMIT

Sometimes we stand at the base of the mountain (our career) and we see the summit. We want to be there right now. We want to accomplish a lifetime of work in less than a year. But what we don't see is the beauty and challenge of the climb. What we don't see is the overall journey and realize that it is long and arduous. We just want the fulfillment of the summit. But what happens at the summit? Celebration and reflection. And that doesn't last forever. When that is over, we realize that we want to climb again. We don't want it to be over. Think about those people who come out of retirement after a long and successful career. By focusing on the climb, our life, career, and personal progress are more enjoyable. And when you enjoy something, you often get there faster! Concentrate on the climb and not the summit.

HEART

How will you serve the world? What does the world need that your talent can provide? What do people need that you can help them with? Everything else is just smoke and mirrors. Believe you have what it takes, because you do.

Your time is limited. Don't waste it. Don't let the voice of other people's opinions drown out your own inner heart. Have the courage to seek what you truly want to become. Here's to your greatness and to becoming a **HAIR BOSS.**